Vignettes...

The story of my life

by

Saul Frechtel

©
2013

Blue Logic Publication
http://bluelogic.us
All rights reserved © 2013
by
Saul Frechtel

No part of this book may be reproduced or transmitted in any form or by any means, graphic, electronic, or mechanical, including photocopying, recording, taping, or by an information storage retrieval system, without permission in writing from the publisher.

ISBN 978-0-9769732-9-4

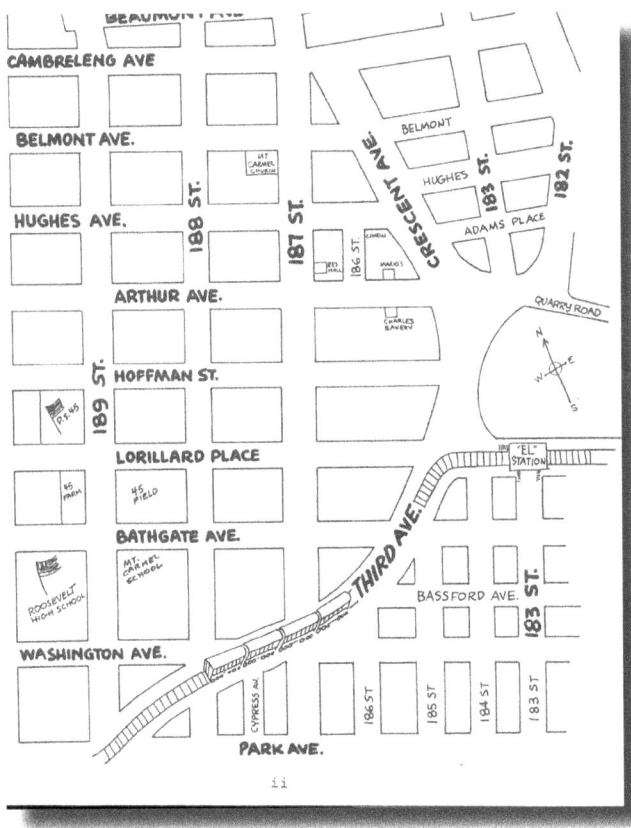

Fordham in the Bronx

Vignettes...

Vignettes[1]

---

1 The diminutive of *vigne* for vineyard, *vignette* is an Old French word meaning literally "vine tendrils". Originally referring inside English circles to the ornamental design bordering a picture frame, with the invention of the camera the word came to mean a small photographic portrait with blurry edges. Then in the 1880s its current meaning began to spread: A short literary sketch, long enough to tell a story, short enough to evoke laughter or a smile. That's what these stories are -- vignettes to evoke laughter and smiles -- from a dear friend and mentor to so many of us.

Editor

The story of my life

Mother – Part One

I must have been five years old when we lived in an Italian neighborhood called *Fordham in the Bronx* at 183rd Street and Bathgate Avenue.

When I asked my mother, *What am I?* she said that I was a good boy. I repeated the question and she replied that I was a very good boy.

My next query was – *Am I Italian?* My mother then said – *So that is what this is all about. No, you are not Italian. You are a Jew.*

With that response, I ran down the stairs and with a loud voice I echoed *I am a Jew, I am a Jew* all the way to the building's front steps and onto the street, where many neighborhood kids were gathered. One of the older boys, who may have been six or seven years old said – in an equally loud voice – *OK Jew – get the ball – you're holding up the game.*

Vignettes...

Mother - Part Two

Not much older than five years old I somehow managed to climb to the roof of a house, which was probably two stories high. Looking down over the roof I could see a crowd of people gathering below, family members and friends, growing anxious by the minute about my safety and intentions. *Call his mother! Somebody get his mother right away!* someone shouted. Some minutes later my mother arrived. Elbowing her way to the front of the crowd, she looked up and said, *Well, he figured out how to climb up there, now he can figure out how to climb down. I'm going home.* She left.

I climbed down.

The story of my life

Mother – Part Three

It was 1928 when I was about six years old, as was my cousin Lilly; and we both lived on Clay Avenue near 174th street in the Bronx. Starting school at P.S. 70 was the task at hand for the two of us. All four parents were either at work or on their way. My mother was the last one left to gather me and Lilly, which she did by taking us to the corner near our building and pointing out that 174th street was the street for us to walk onto. This was a very busy and congested high-traffic street.

My mother pointed down 174th street and said, *The school is about ten blocks that way. Ask Molcha* [Lilly's mother who was in her butcher store across the street from the school] *to walk you across 174th street.* Then she was gone.

Vignettes...

Lily and I walked and walked and walked, joining other children, some of whom had a parent to guide them. It was most obvious -- to me at least -- what we had to do when we got to school, which was a beehive of activity with children, parents, and teachers.

We sorted out what looked like a teacher and simply asked, *Where is first grade?* Of course, we found it and settled into our seats. *We were on our way!* Lilly and I had registered ourselves into first grade.

The story of my life

Baby Sister
Fourteen Years Old – 1938

My "baby sister" was fourteen years old (1938) and became ill. Our family physician, who was a relative and normally was an obstetrician, in his enthusiasm to help us had her admitted into Willard Parker Hospital located on East 16th street and the East River in Manhattan where they treated contagious diseases. The High School that I attended (Stuyvesant) was about four blocks away and very close to the Hospital. This made it easy for me to visit her, except that I was never allowed into the building because of the contagious aspect. Ultimately, I found the room that she was in and through a partially open window I could speak to her. Her immediate request was for me to get her out of that hospital. Between us we had hatched a scheme to accomplish this.

Vignettes...

She suggested that I enlist our cousin Lilly to get street clothes, including shoes, to her. Lilly went to our mother to gather the clothes and I directed Lilly to an exterior door that only opened from inside the building. Some employees continuously exited through this door, and at the right moment, Lilly walked into the building and into sis' room. Lily helped dress her and they both walked out of the building. Nobody came looking for my sister and that was that. We accomplished the "grand escape," with the help of our mother who always let us make our own decisions.

The story of my life

Briarwood Baseball Club

Our Briarwood Baseball Club is a study of how neighborhood sandlot teams formed and functioned, that predated Little Leagues. There wasn't any parental interest or interference and were completely self-managed and directed. We had scheduled games, obtained permits for the use of city-owned fields, and made in-house travel arrangements. In 1936, I was thirteen years old, was voted captain of our team, and kept it all together and functioning.

The original core of the Briarwoods came from a neighborhood in Queens called Jamaica. The Abrevaya family – parents, four children and an aged, deaf grandmother – moved from a large house to a prominent apartment in the Bronx – with a magnificent view. The oldest son, Leon, was the ball player and the initial impetus for the Briarwood baseball club, and it grew from there.

Vignettes...

*Saul, team captain:
first row, middle*

The story of my life

We had dues, bought uniforms and equipment, and amazingly functioned with little friction. Actually, we showed the other neighborhood teams how to do it.

This was truly a success story, and we went on for years, harmoniously. There were about thirty of us, boys and girls; and for the most part, stuck together to this very day.

Vignettes...

Crescas' Family

Victor Crescas' father was what today we would call *a Power Broker*. I did not know it when I was a teenager, but he was a remarkable man in a remarkable era. He was the Maître d' of a prestigious club – the Versailles Night Club at 151 East 50th Street in Manhattan. The premises was restyled and redesigned in 1946 and, along with Victor, I was in the club many times. In 1950, Edith Piaf, the French Chanteuse was featured and inadvertently I and my future wife were guests of Victor's father, who was known as Robert.

Robert was also acquainted with J. Edgar Hoover who were close to one another. In 1938, Victor, myself, and our friend Boris Friedman were all attending high school together. We decided to go to Washington D.C. for our Christmas break. Robert engaged the F.B.I. (Federal Bureau of Investigation) to host our trip.

The story of my life

When we got to Washington, we called a prearranged chauffeur and a car to escort us anywhere we wanted to go. Our first stop was the F.B.I. building, where we were ushered into J. Edgar Hoover's big office (while he was on vacation in Florida), where we all took turns sitting in his chair. There wasn't a single sheet of paper visible, but there were adjoining offices with many file cabinets. We went through offices where our finger prints and photos were taken. There was a sound proof shooting gallery, and one surprising area after another. Our escort (the chauffeur) took us to the U.S. Supreme Court where we freely walked through the offices and court rooms. The Treasury Building, with huge presses printing money was impressive. George Washington's home at Mount Vernon was memorable, as was his birthplace at Colonial Beach, VA, about 50 miles south of his home. It was a whirlwind tour and none of us had a camera. Boris became Duggan by eating donuts at a bakery called "Duggan's"

Vignettes...

and from that trip on we, and all of our friends, called him Duggan.

Victor's father managed to get Victor into Stuyvesant High School, without merit, where all the students were high achievers and had exclusively passed a rigid examination. Victor was admitted and was given passing grades – although he was a lackluster poor student, I do believe that he actually ultimately graduated and received a diploma.

Robert arranged a job for Victor in an Architect's office, which was short-lived because Victor did not have the intellect for faking work in a technical field and could not advance without a formal education.

Somewhere around 1942, when all of our friends were reporting to Draft Boards and going into the various military services, Victor's father managed to get Victor into the U.S. Coast Guard. He was stationed in an office in lower

The story of my life

Manhattan and lived in a hotel, where he had his meals and had money for many expenses, and where he sat out the war. This maneuver by Robert Crescas was amazing to me and all I could say was Wow! Particularly when in 1944, I went into the army and was sent to the Pacific Theater of Operation, and didn't come back home for two years.

By war's end, his father got him a job selling paint for a large manufacturer, along with an automobile and an expense account, where he actually excelled. Ultimately, Victor managed to start a competitive enterprise manufacturing paint spray can products. He was distinctly successful in this taxing business. Then he had a heart attack and died at the top of his game. His father predeceased him and never saw him as an ultimate success.

Vignettes...

High School

Stuyvesant High School: A population of high achievers, who were required to pass an entrance exam.

I started 9th grade by capturing the one and only math (Algebra) medal – which was quite an accomplishment when considering that there were 1,000 of us in the 9th grade. In the 10th grade, 1937, I became ill, was hospitalized, and failed all of my classes. From then on, I doubled up on my classes and audited many courses. My aim was to ultimately get through the 12th grade and graduate in 1940, on the original schedule. The only other outstanding achievement was scoring the highest physics New York State-wide Regents examination test.

The math and physics accomplishments were honored at graduation on the stage at Carnegie Hall and my parents, who were perpetually working were not there – only my baby sister attended to cheer me on.

College

Admission to the Engineering School at the City College of New York was not necessarily a slam dunk, because of my bizarre high school record, where I lost, and then made up, a year's time.

1940 and 1941 were two difficult years (Freshman & Sophomore), because I inadvertently was not prepared to study the way I had to. Only when I reached my Junior year did I hit my stride and I became a B student, which was amazing and encouraging, and ultimately where I belonged.

World War II, the Draft Board, and the School were tumultuous days that were fiercely competitive and I did graduate on schedule and then entered the U.S. Army. The Draft Board got the school grading system changed from Letters – A, B, C, & D – to a numerical score, right down to three decimals; such as 82.167, etc. Every student was positioned on the list and was shown in order of their grade.

Vignettes...

Each six months, the list was posted with a selection line drawn across the page. If you were above the line, your draft status was extended; if not, then you were no longer draft deferred. I survived this selection process for two years, until I completed Engineering School in 1944.

I ultimately learned that the U.S. Government was building a labor pool of engineers for development of the Atomic Bomb, and I was in the pool. This was what made my schooling so competitive to graduate and then enter the military.

The engineering education served me for a life time of constant employment and high earnings and was well worth the enormous effort.

Many 2:00 and 3:00 am study times were initiated by my baby sister, whose task it was to get me up so I could get to the books.

Babcock & Wilson

In 1956-57, I was employed by Babcock & Wilcox as a designer of steam generation plants, which stood about twelve stories high. They were a very aggressive company and moved many employees around Florida. I wasn't enamored by too much movement and doing design work, and left their employment.

My primary interest was in doing contracting and sought work with a general contracting company.

Vignettes...

Contracting – Nat Harrison Associates
Chapter 1
Grand Bahama Island: Bahamas

We were doing a job, a relatively small office building one-story, approximately 2,000 sq. ft. – about five to six miles from the nearest local native town. The road from the town to the job site was very poor. Ruts, pot holes, etc., and difficult for a vehicle. We had an old minimum pickup truck that our superintendent used. It required a lot of maintenance and the boss was reluctant to send a better truck to this job because it would not be a better vehicle for very long. After much discussion back in Miami (the home office), it was decided to send about fifteen bicycles to the town so that we didn't have to send our truck to pick up the construction crew of about fifteen men from the town to the job site. After delivering the bicycles, the next morning the superintendent was waiting at the job site for the crew.

The story of my life

After a ten-minute wait, he got into his truck to go to the town to look for the crew. He met them on the road – walking on the road towards the job site. They all had a bicycle that they were wheeling along the road. When asked why they were walking the bicycles, instead of riding them, it was because none of them knew how to ride a bicycle.

We ultimately finished the job with the old truck used as transportation.

Vignettes...

Contracting – Nat Harrison Associates
Chapter 2

Mobilizing the materials in Miami for the Grand Bahama Island office building, for shipment to the job site was unique because it was a relatively small job for our Company.

We rented an empty warehouse, approximately 4,000 sq. ft. and had all materials delivered to the premises. Concurrently, we commenced building plywood containers, approximately 8'x4'x4', which we packed with assorted materials: plumbing, electrical, ceilings, etc. The plywood was expensive and thick because we intended to ultimately reuse all of it in the construction of the building to meet all of the U.S. Navy specifications.

The story of my life

Generally, it was our intent for the plywood to be used initially as crates, forms for the concrete footings, then sheathing for the roof, and finally siding for the exterior walls. The use and reuse of the plywood was ultimately very economical.

A dispute arose with the U.S. Navy (owners of the project) and their inspector. When the construction was complete – were the plywood sheets still considered new or used? Two or three meetings were required at the U.S. Navy office at Patrick Air Force Base in Florida. Our argument was that the plywood was purchased new and met all specifications of the project's contract. We prevailed and all parties were satisfied.

Vignettes...

Contracting – Nat Harrison Associates
Chapter 3

The year was 1959. We were doing a job in Cutler Maine, building a very low frequency radio station for the U.S. Navy's Polaris submarine program. There were three such installations in the world. One was in Maine, a second one in North Western England, and the third in Western Australia. The station in Maine covered an area of about a mile in diameter and 1,000 feet high. The electrical array consisted of cables of about two inches in diameter and on occasion had to be maintained by lowering all of it to the ground, repaired, and then raised back into place. There were a set of winches that were mounted on shorter 200-foot high towers that were utilized to accomplish the maintenance. These towers were also furnished by us, which were designed by a U.S. Engineer

The story of my life

in Atlanta, GA and ultimately fabricated in Italy because there was a steel strike in the U.S. and we could not purchase any domestic steel. Since I was the only Engineer in our Company with a bit of knowledge of Italian, I was chosen to work with the steel fabricators in their office in Milan, Italy.

Myself, and an American steel designer from Atlanta reviewed the drawings and by both of us being on one premises, we could efficiently pass drawings from one office to another, eliminating the mailings between us entirely. Myself and the other American were given abutting offices. We quickly learned that the Italian design staff had about a three-hour lunch hour and worked in the evenings to fill out their day. Since this was an odd arrangement for us, we reorganized our schedule to have a 12 noon to 1:00 pm lunch hour and kept to our normal eight-hour day. There was a kitchen and dining room in the lower floors, where various executives were accommodated so that we were not a burden on

Vignettes...

their facilities. They gave us a dining room on our floor and the first day, a waitress brought us some soup, as our first course.

However, a fly also came up from the kitchen and we put the emptied soup plates on the window sill to attract the fly. When the waitress arrived with our pasta course, she started to gather our soup plates to take back to the kitchen. At this point, I explained to her, in my best Italian, to leave the soup plates on the window sill to keep the fly engaged so that we could finish our lunches without the annoyance of the fly. She complied with our request and went back to the kitchen, with the story that these Americans were so generous that they were concerned that a fly should also have something to eat.

The story of my life

Vehicle Assembly Building (VAB) Kennedy Space Center – 1966 Opening

One of the world's biggest single story structures, by volume. Cape Canaveral, Florida.

Contains four of the largest exterior doors in the world (each one is 456 feet high). The lower portion is similar to airplane hanger doors. Upper portion is similar to venetian blind stacking.

We didn't design these doors, nor did we build them. Our contribution was the erection, which entailed many innovated procedures by our staff. This we accomplished with great skill and proficiency.

Vignettes...

Lake Charles, Louisiana

In *Lake Charles, Louisiana,* we did a sophisticated ship loading facility which included loading and unloading very large grain storage silos in soils that were swamps. The challenges to build in these conditions led to many disputes, meetings, change orders, and compromises. We ultimately completed this work to every ones satisfaction.

The story of my life

My Sister and My Brother-In-Law, Morris

Morris is currently (2012) in an Elder Care facility in the Bronx, New York, which we know as an *Old Age Home,* where he is an Alzheimer victim under Hospice care.

I and my sister visited Morris many months ago and joined him and a group of other visitors and residents for lunch.

There was a particular woman named Edith who took a shine to me, rearranged the seating of several diners and wound up in a chair next to me.

She started the conversation with me: *Where are you from?* she asked. I replied, *California. Well,* she continued, *Let's start over. Where were you born?* I replied, *Right here in the Bronx, in a hospital*

Vignettes...

that is still in existence and is now known as the Bronx Lebanon Hospital Center on Fulton Avenue. With that bit of trivia revealed, she said, *So was I – and that is where I know you from.*

To this very day, my sister encounters Edith, who always questions Sis about me and my welfare, and when am I coming again to visit.

Saul Frechtel

The story of my life

*Saul, 91
2013*

www.ingramcontent.com/pod-product-compliance
Ingram Content Group UK Ltd.
Pitfield, Milton Keynes, MK11 3LW, UK
UKHW022121230426
12048UKWH00011BA/639